Cross-Cultural Education
Teaching Toward
a Planetary Perspective

# CROSS-CULTURAL EDUCATION

Teaching Toward
a Planetary Perspective
By Robert L. Williams

The Curriculum Series

National Education Association
Washington, D.C.

**NOTE**

The opinions expressed in this publication should not be construed as representing the policy or position of the National Education Association. Materials published as part of the *NEA Curriculum Series* are intended to be discussion documents for teachers who are concerned with specialized interests of the profession.

**Library of Congress Cataloging in Publication Data**

Williams, Robert L     1937–
  Cross-cultural education.

  (The Curriculum series)
  Bibliography: p.
  1. Intercultural education—United States.
I. Title.    II. Series.
LC1099.W54      370.19'6'0973      77-10484
ISBN 0-8106-1705-6
ISBN 0-8106-1704-8 pbk.

# CONTENTS

*To*
*Those Persons*
*Whose Inquiries and Insights*
*Provided the Spark*
*for the Conceptualization*
*of This Book*

*and*
*To All Who Would Share*
*in a Common Circle*
*of Human Understanding*
*and Peace*

# PREFACE

This book was written with three basic objectives in mind. The first objective was to point out to educators the critical need for providing every American student with a polycultural education. Polycultural education is defined as those educational experiences which the school provides that enable students to better appreciate and value their own ethnocultural dimensions and the ethnocultural dimensions of others. Every American is polycultural, having many ethnocultural dimensions, for example, white-Irish-Pentecostal-Yankee, Native American-Seminole-female-Floridian-urban, black-southern-Protestant-rural, Chinese-bilingual-Californian-male, Mexican-multilingual-Catholic-midwestern. A collective understanding and valuing by every American of these diverse dimensions could be a powerful force for moving Americans to higher levels of human understanding. And higher levels of human understanding are needed if we are to resolve many of the human conflicts which threaten the chances of humanistic equity and peace.

A second objective of this book was to point out the responsibility American education has for educating its student clientele to high levels of international ethnocultural literacy. That responsibility ought to include the offering of well-conceived, well-implemented, and well-evaluated polycultural programs.

The third objective of this report was to suggest to educational institutions step-by-step organizational approaches for developing and implementing polycultural educational programs.

I have taken the liberty to coin the term "polycultural," instead of using the often-used term "multicultural." This was done to take the issue of ethnocultural education beyond the limitations of race, as historically has been the case. It is time that education begin the task of teaching other ethnocultural dimensions, such as, religion, geographic residence, gender, political view, socioeconomic status. All these dimensions are interrelated and are increasingly coming into play in the world's drama of human survival. The election of Jimmy Carter to the Presidency of the United States of America brought the power of polyculturism into sharp focus. President

Carter was elected through an effective coalition of white southern Baptists, northern and southern blacks, regional rural populists, feminists, ethnic blue-collar workers, Jews, Irish, and many disenchanted Republicans. Historians may recall the 1976 election as the year Americans of the North, South, East and West united their diverse ethnocultural dimensions for a common collective cause, our nation's healing.

But America, and American education in particular, has far to go. After more than three decades of marches, protests, and racial hostilities we still find ourselves mired in the manifestations of dehumanization: racial conflicts in desegregating schools, Molotov cocktails through the windows of black neighbors, rapidly separating central cities and suburban communities, rioting in penal institutions, rioting on our military installations. These ugly patterns of human conflict can be seen day after day, year after year the world over. We are witness to the hostilities between Protestants and Catholics in Ireland, in West Asia we see raging conflicts between the Moslem-Arab countries and Israel, and in East Asia we are witness to a long-standing ideological conflict between the People's Republic of China and the Soviet Union. We sense the volcanic eruption about to occur between the blacks and whites of South Africa. We observe our own nation and find patterns of prejudice among whites, blacks, Native Americans, Mexican Americans and other oppressed ethnocultural groups. These are a few of many reasons that underscore a need for polycultural education.

But where, when, and how do we begin our systematic quest to break century-old patterns of human conflict based on ethnocultural considerations? I believe the logical place to begin resolution of these problems is through our educational institutions. We must institutionalize systemic problem-solving approaches now if we expect to leave a legacy of lasting human understanding and peace to the generations to come.

In arguing the need for polycultural education, I am advocating a comprehensive institutionalized interdisciplinary approach to curriculum development. I am not advocating more of the same of what has been labeled multicultural or pluralistic educational approaches to curriculum. What I am advocating is the development of curricula that helps each student develop an international ethnocultural perspective: a frame of reference beyond the anthropologically-derived phenomena we have come to know as race. In presenting the case for polycultural education, I am addressing more than just the traditional potpourri of disconnected ethnocultural hero-worship oriented history courses. Polycultural education will be addressed in this volume as both process and product, interrelated and integral to the total educational curriculum of the organization. The emphasis in this report, however, will be limited to the administrative development and maintenance of a process as a means to achieving the desired end product: a polycultural curriculum. No attempt will be made in this book to address specific day-to-day classroom teaching materials, media, or methodologies. That ground has already been thoroughly plowed by scholars—Dr. James A. Banks, Dr. Albert Swartz, Dr. Jean Grambs, and others.

I have presented the case for polycultural education. We have the choice and the challenge to make polycultural education a reality for America's most precious resource, our children and youth. Although this in itself would not be enough to cure centuries of rampant racism and other dehumanizing "isms" that perpetuate world conflict, it could be a major step in the process of arresting a disease. Perhaps the urgency of the challenge was best reflected in the following statement by a long-time proponent of apartheid, Rhodesia's Prime Minister Ian Smith, "We live in a world of rapid change and if we are to survive in such a world, we must be prepared to adapt ourselves to change".[1]

There must be change if the phenomena of international human understanding and world peace are ever to be realities for people on this planet. And change will occur if people are re-educated to new levels of understanding one another. Hopefully, in our energy-exchanges with one another, we will come to deeper understandings of ourselves, and with that new self-awareness find better ways to live on our ever-shrinking planetary world-neighborhood. Polycultural education could be one of the keys to better life chances in our world-neighborhood. The phenomenon of polycultural understanding cannot, and must not, be abandoned to chance.

Robert L. Williams

---

[1]Rigert, Joe. "Rhodesia's Whites No Longer Talk of Holding Out." *Minneapolis Star,* November 21, 1976.

# POLYCULTURAL EDUCATION: MAKING IT HAPPEN

A multiplicity of terminologies has been used to define educational approaches for a pluralistic society. It is unfortunate that these approaches have the melting-pot theory as their premise. Polycultural education rejects the melting-pot theory and its subliminal racist objective of melting away the cultures of one ethnocultural group into the cultures of another.

Polycultural education, from a planetary perspective, might be voiced as education to enhance and preserve all the ethnocultures of humanity. It embraces the idea of multicultural education as proposed by the American Association Colleges for Teacher Education:

> Multicultural education is education which values cultural pluralism. Multicultural education rejects the view that schools should seek to melt away cultural differences on the view that schools should merely tolerate cultural pluralism . . . cultural pluralism rejects both assimilation and separatism as ultimate goals. Instead, multicultural education affirms that schools should be oriented toward the cultural enrichment of all children and youth through programs pointed to the preservation and extension of cultural alternatives.[2]

Cultural pluralism, multicultural education, and polycultural education all embrace two common ideals: (1) A state of equal, mutual supportive coexistence between ethnocultural groups, and (2) one planet of people of diverse physical and cultural characteristics. Basic to the acceptance of these ideals is the belief that every person respects his or her ethnocultural identity and extends the same respect for the cultures of others. This position suggests certain implications for educators and educational institutions. Harry Passow brings these implications into sharp focus:

---

[2]The American Association of Colleges for Teacher Education. "Statement to Serve as a Guide for Multicultural Education." *AACTE Bulletin,* 1974.

While schools must certainly do a far more effective job in the basic skills areas, an education for a culturally pluralistic society must have a broader focus which deals with affective and cognitive development, with personal and interpersonal skills, and with an understanding by the individual of who he is and how he relates to others.[3]

Polycultural education has been defined in this book as that process or that product which enables a student to achieve higher-level ethnic, cultural world perspectives. We are defining polycultural education as both product and process. It is a process in that there is intellectual interaction among students, teachers, and parents. It is a product in that there is a specific program design (curriculum) which prescribes specific learning activities involving students, teachers, and parents.

But polycultural education, more than either process or product, should be viewed as a liberating tool, which enables one to be more effective in eradicating the conditions of oppression from society. Sekou Toure, President of Guinea, underscores the potential of polyculturalism as a liberating tool in his definition of culture:

By culture we mean all the material and immaterial works of art and science, plus knowledge, manners, education, mode of thought, behaviors, and attitudes accumulated by the people both through and by virtue of their struggle for freedom from the hell and domination of Nature. We also include the result of their efforts to destroy the deviationist politics—social systems of domination and exploitation through the productive processes of social life.[4]

A polycultural curriculum is defined as a set of prescribed student experiences provided through the school and world communities. This definition transcends the traditional definition of curriculum, derived from its Latin origin, meaning a course of study. This is because the world today is an open classroom. Television has made possible the direct study of other world cultures. Educational institutions need only to tap this great reservoir of knowledge to make polycultural curriculum a reality for every American student.

---

[3]Passow, Harry. "New Curriculum for Ethnic Schools." *Equal Opportunity Review,* June 1975.

[4]Toure, Sekou. "A Dialectical Approach to Culture." *Pan-Africanism.* (Edited by Robert Chrisman and Nathan Hare.) New York: The Bobbs-Merrill Co., Inc., 1974. p. 55.

In making polycultural curriculum happen, several precepts come to mind:

## Precept 1: The Polycultural Curriculum Should Delineate a Prescribed Set of Educational Experiences

Such a prescribed set of educational experiences should be derived from: (1) Clearly delineated objectives, (2) content authenticated from the racial, ethnic, and cultural clientele served, (3) methodologies appropriate to the racial, ethnic, and cultural clientele served, (4) contemporary and historically validated materials, and (5) a student-teacher-parent evaluation process.
Noted educator Dr. James A. Banks states:

> Vital ethnic studies programs should enable students to derive valid generalizations about the characteristics of all America's ethnic groups, and to learn how they are alike and different, in both their past and present experiences . . . to help students develop, what I call, ethnic literacy and to grasp the significance of ethnicity within American life, ethnic studies must focus on higher level concepts and generalizations and not discreet facts about isolated heroes and contributions.[5]

## Precept 2: The Polycultural Curriculum Should Include the Discussion of Contemporary International Topics as a Means of Teaching Concepts and Generalizations

The recent oil embargo in West Asia and its international sociopolitical consequences is an excellent subject for classroom discussions at the secondary level. A word of caution: The sustained interests of the students will be in direct proportion to the interest-raising content in the materials and the enthusiasm of the teacher.

## Precept 3: A Polycultural Curriculum Should Provide the Staff, as a Team, the Flexibility to Plan Interdisciplinary Team-Teaching Approaches

Team-teaching approaches should be planned around contempo-

---

[5]Banks, James A. "Teaching for Ethnic Literacy: A Comparative Approach." *Social Education* 37:743, 747; December 1973.

rary topics, issues, ideas, modes of inquiry, and generalizations. These should connect subject matter areas such as science, language arts, mathematics, and social studies. For example, the oil embargo might be the connecting topic for an interdisciplinary team-approach involving the economics class, the language arts class, the chemistry class, and the political science class. The economics class might address the nomenclature of the international economic system, exploring how it is possible that a few Western nations control the flow of goods and services around the world. A mode of inquiry might center around the statement that three million whites in Africa enjoy a very high standard of living, while fifteen million blacks on the same continent exist essentially in economic slavery. The language arts class might explore the reasons why English is the international language or examine the influence of English in promulgating European values and attitudes among non-European nations. The chemistry class might address the consequences of the oil embargo on the reduction of fertilizer production in Western and African nations. The political science class might explore the sociopolitical impact of the oil embargo on American multinational corporations operating in newly decolonized countries such as Angola and Mozambique.

*Precept 4: The Polycultural Curriculum Should Be an Integral Part of the Organization's Total Educational Effort*

*Precept 5: The Polycultural Curriculum Should Provide for Thorough Classroom Discussions of Ethnocultural Differences, and Ethnocultural Similarities*

In the classroom discussions of ethnocultural differences, the students should begin to explore and clarify these self-directed questions:

- Who am I?
- What are my ethnic, racial, and cultural roots?
- How can I meet my sociopolitical responsibilities as a citizen?
- How can I prevail over the conditions that occasion my oppression?

Ethnocultural role models should be discussed as they relate to cultural differences. The students of an English literature class might explore the works of Langston Hughes. In focusing on ethnocultural differences, the students would be interested in Langston Hughes as black poet. Classroom discussions would include an analysis of black culture as it influenced his writing style, syntax, use of black idiom, and other literary dimensions that characterize his works. In classroom discussions on ethnocultural similarities the students would explore the profile and the works of Langston Hughes as poet. Here the students would read and recite the works of Hughes but focus on the literary genius that is characteristic of all great poets.

## Precept 6: The Polycultural Curriculum Should Provide Opportunities for Teachers and Students to Develop Personal-Interest-Focused Ethnocultural Curricula Materials

Personal-interest ethnocultural curricula materials have great potential for teaching and learning. One example of these materials is the episode unit. Episode units are short story vignettes about the everyday experiences of the students. The subject for the episode unit should be selected by the students in collaboration with the teacher. Episode units can be developed around such themes as:

- What it is like to walk in the shoes of a Mexican migrant worker.
- The day-to-day experience of a white family in Appalachia.
- A black family in a predominantly white neighborhood.
- A Native American family in a large city.

Development of episode units can be a rewarding experience for students, teachers, and parents. One ethnic community group in an urban school system asked to be involved with students and teachers in their search for validated historical background information that was to be included in the episode units. The ethnic group expressed concern that well-researched historically validated materials be used since poorly validated materials, they felt, would only serve to reinforce negative stereotypes. The search yielded unexpected positive results. A university in Ohio was found to have the world's most extensive collection of ethnic materials for the particular ethnic group under study. Once the ethnic community group received the background materials requested from the university in Ohio, a series of study-discussions were scheduled. The ethnic group after studying the materials, invited the classroom teacher into the group sessions. Specific concerns and suggestions from the group were shared with the classroom teacher. The teacher/student-ethnic group involvement in addition to improving communications between these two groups facilitated the ethnic group's general support for the episode units developed. Harry Passow underscores a sound rationale for the use of episode materials:

> By validating the child's experiences and feelings, the school tells the child that he knows something and that he is worth something.[6]

## Precept 7: Human Resources Should Be Properly Allocated to Develop Polycultural Curricula Materials

Organizations considering the development of polycultural curricula materials such as the episode unit should allocate the necessary human resources to accomplish the task. Organizations should identify a team of professionals, preferably persons already in the organization. These persons should be assigned full-time role responsibilities for the design, development, field-testing, implementation, and evaluation of polycultural curricula materials. All persons assigned such responsibilities should be knowledgeable of the following materials:

- *The Mis-Education of the Negro* by Carter G. Woodson
- *Teaching Strategies for the Social Studies: Inquiry, Valuing & Decision-Making* by James A. Banks
- *Teaching the Black Experience: Methods & Materials* by James A. Banks
- *The Oriental Americans* by H. Brett Melendy
- *Occupied America: The Chicano's Struggle Toward Liberation* by Rudy Acuña
- *New World Beginnings: Indian Cultures in the Americas* by Olivia Vlahos
- *Strangers in the Land: Patterns of American Nationalism 1860–1925* by John Higham
- *The Rise of the Unmeltable Ethnics* by Michael Novak.
- *Roots* by Alex Haley

---

[6]*Passow.*

## Precept 8: The Polycultural Curriculum Should Provide Opportunities for Classroom Discussions of Contemporary Leadership Role Models

Hero-study should be used as a means to classroom discussions of contemporary leadership role models. The emphasis in such discussions should be on the methods employed by these role models to improve the human condition for oppressed peoples and society in general. A few issues are suggested for class discussions:

- The implications of the lettuce and grape boycotts for Chicano migrant workers.
- The implications of affirmative action and seniority for oppressed minorities.
- Who is providing leadership to provide better housing for oppressed people?
- The impact of black mayors on American politics.
- What should be the position of oppressed people on metropolitanism (condition of suburban political control of central city government)?
- Should oppressed people be concerned about the medical-science technique of cloning?

Topic issues such as these can help each student to develop higher level ethnocultural world perspectives.

## Precept 9: A Polycultural Curriculum Should Provide Learning Experiences To Enhance the Ethnocultural Self-Concept of Every Student

Educators should remember as a guiding principle that we are first, teachers of students—all students. Hence, great preparation and care should be taken in the selection and use of polycultural curricula materials. Classroom discussions should foster unity and not division among ethnocultural groups.

The teacher should at the same time cultivate in all students higher levels of ethnocultural awareness. Educators and educational organizations have a responsibility for providing their students with opportunities to achieve higher level ethnocultural perspectives. These opportunities can be provided through a polycultural curriculum. It is time that educators begin making it happen!

# ORGANIZING THE POLYCULTURAL CURRICULUM

A quality polycultural program will include in its organizational structure:

1. A concise organizational statement of philosophy
2. A clear delineation of goals and objectives
3. A delineation of the assigned tasks and responsibilities necessary to achieve the stated goals and objectives
4. The timetable for achievement of the goals and objectives
5. The process and procedures to be followed in carrying out the assigned tasks
6. The criteria to be used in the assessment/evaluation of the program
7. The budgetary resources allocated to implement the program.

The development of a sound philosophic organizational statement should be considered the first and perhaps most critical step in the organizing process. This is because philosophies, in addition to influencing the behaviors of professionals in the organization, have also served to influence the organizational development of goals and objectives. Historically, organizations have generally ignored the need to develop goals and objectives designed to help students develop polycultural world perspectives. And in too many instances where goals and objectives were developed, these were developed on faulty philosophic rationale. One example that comes to mind is the way many educational institutions have attempted to address the issue of religious observances in the schools.

Time after time, and holiday after holiday, educators and educational institutions have implemented sectarian observances, in violation of the principle of separation of church and state. With the U.S. Supreme Court decision, *Abington* v. *Schempp–Murray,* June 1963, the Court ruled that public school educators can teach about religions through the academic curriculum. A school may sponsor the study about religions but may not teach a religion or impose a particular view. And here is where many educational institutions have erred. In holding religious observances where attendance is required of all students and where the musical selections presented reflect one dominant religious view, a subliminal goal-objective icon is projected. In some schools that icon is Anglo-Saxon Protestant. In some schools that icon is Anglo-Saxon Catholic. But what about the other religious views represented in those same schools? No single monolithic icon (whether of race, religion, or any other ethnocultural dimensions) should be presumed by educators to be a universal model on which to develop curricula offerings for all ethnocultural groups.

Any philosophic statement on which a polycultural program is developed should clearly state the organization's position on the issue of cultural pluralism. There has been unnecessary confusion in the ranks of educators over definitions of pluralism. Too often poorly-conceived multicultural programs have resulted in confusion over definitions. The American Association of Colleges for Teacher Education has defined multicultural education as education which values pluralism. It is interesting to note that the issue of pluralism has never been considered important enough to be defined by the diverse ethnocultural groups of the nation. Pluralism has been defined by too many educational institutions with the notion of ethnocultural minorities being absorbed into the culture of the predominant European culture. But if the same definition derived from the majority group were applied to the world at large, Europeans would be absorbed into the predominant world culture that is non-European. This is not to argue the desirability of one position over the other. What is needed is a closer examination by educational  institutions of the ways in which definitions are developed. These definitions should reflect more equitably the student ethnocultural groups served by educational institutions.

Great care should be taken in developing the organizational philosophic statement since it is, in principle, the organization's first expression of formal commitment to the implementation of a polycultural curriculum. It is also the basis for the organizational framework on which the polycultural curriculum will be developed. But here a caution is advisable: organizational structure must never be allowed to become an end in itself, for that would undermine the humanistic rationale for polycultural education. Organizational structures should be developed to transcend the limitations too often inherent in organizational charts and PERTS. In the final analysis, these are at best conceptual images on charts. But images on charts are secondary in importance. The most essential ingredient for implementing polycultural programs is people!

The talents of students, teachers, administrators, parents, and lay citizens should be put to work in developing the organization's philosophic position for polycultural education. However, the adoption of a philosophic statement by a board of education will not in itself, insure the implementation of that position. A statement of policy (based on the philosophic position of the organization) will need to be developed by the organization. The regulations will be needed to insure the implementation of the organization's policy. A strong policy statement can facilitate ethnocultural sensitivities within organizations, particularly if committees meet to evaluate and recommend learning materials for adoption by the organization. A strong policy statement can register a clear message to textbook publishers and other educational suppliers. Current nationwide conflicts over which learning materials shall or shall not be used in schools are likely to escalate until there are clear federal, state, and local institutional policies for ethnocultural education.

The philosophic statements of organizations will vary from organization to organization, depending upon the needs of the student ethnocultural groups served. But every polycultural curriculum should address such fundamental issues as the roles and achievements of ethnocultural groups and their contributions to American and world history. Every polycultural curriculum should address the presentation of factual information on the human injustices perpetrated. Every polycultural curriculum should be designed to dispel in the teaching-learning process racist/sexist myths and racist/sexist stereotypes!

Generally speaking, an organization's commitment to the implementation of polycultural curricula will be reflected in a number of ways. The obvious signs to the would-be skeptic are the following:

## 1. *Clearly Delineated Goals and Objectives*
### *An Example:*

A polycultural program will be established for school district $\underline{Y}$ to educate students for life in a polycultural community, a polycultural nation, and a polycultural planet.

An example of a Statement of Objectives:

a. The polycultural program will focus on grade levels K–12.
b. Content emphasis will be on the life experiences of ethnic groups $\underline{A}$ and $\underline{B}$ for grade one and cultural group $\underline{C}$ for grade seven.
c. An interdisciplinary team approach will be used to focus for a period of $\underline{X}$ weeks to explore contemporary issues as they relate to racial, ethnic, and cultural groups. The subject-area groups to be involved are: chemistry, mathematics, language arts, social studies, history, and political science.
d. A faculty committee will be organized to develop criteria for assessing the polycultural materials and programs for the district.
e. The goals and objectives for polycultural programs will be an integral part of the goals and objectives for the total organization.
f. The polycultural program will serve all students and will involve the total organization staff.
g. Faculty in-service education will be provided to increase faculty competence in the design, implementation, and assessment of polycultural materials.
h. The polycultural program is expected to be fully implemented by $\underline{X}$ date at a cost of $\underline{Y}$ dollars to the organization.

## 2. A Statement of Commitment by the Organization to Develop Relevant Learning Materials

This position suggests the use of minority ethnic teachers in the development of such materials and strongly suggests the involvement of community in the development of such materials. J. Y. Moreland, Area Superintendent, Atlanta Public Schools, underscores this point:

> It has only been recently that we've had textbooks which had pictures to which minority children could relate. But there is still a lack of realness in the books, although this is to be expected because the persons writing these materials have a difficult time writing about something they haven't experienced.[7]

---

[7]Moreland, J. Y. "History Texts Seldom Place Black Feats in Proper Perspective." *Twin City Courier,* February 15, 1974.

## 3. *Establishing a Full-Time Role Position of Coordinator for Polycultural Programs*

The coordinator must be responsible for insuring the developmental aspects of a polycultural curriculum. Once the implementation phase is underway, the program must be monitored to insure the smooth coordination of all program components. Several specific strategies are suggested for a coordinator of polycultural programs:

a. Briefings with the administrative officers (organization staff and planning staff) should focus on the accomplishment of objectives.

b. Coordinating the activities of a staff-appointed steering committee. The steering committee would provide counsel within the organization.

c. Coordinating the activities of *ad hoc* writing committees to develop polycultural materials. The critical variables for the selection of members to a writing committee are philosophic-orientation and function-orientation (task or advisory).

A word of caution—personal conflicts between members on working committees often result in diffused energies, frustration for individuals on the committee, and failure of a committee to accomplish its task. Ideologic antagonists should never be assigned to the same committee. Explosive combinations are: task orientationists and advisory orientationists; decision-making-by-consensus advocates, and those who find it expedient to follow directions already prescribed by others; integrationists and separatists; traditionalists and change-agents; and cultural pluralists and pan-nationalists.

We would underscore the need for caution in the selection of personnel to *ad hoc* working committees. Time and personal commitment of committee members to polycultural education should be the overriding criteria for the selection of personnel to the working committees. Where time is a critical factor for completion of the task, it is imperative that the committee members come in, roll up their sleeves, and get to work! Productivity is diminished when committee members engage in lengthy philosophic arguments and digressions. The coordinator's major function in the working committee is to hold the committee to its task until completion.

The coordinator's role-position must be flexible, and free of the red tape that characterizes traditional organizations. Since the coordinator's role-position is fundamentally a catalyst-for-change position, it is essential that it has enforcement power. This can be accomplished in a number of ways:

    a.  A strong organizational policy statement
    b.  Direct access to the head administrative officer of the organization
    c.  Direct access to other administrators in the organization who have responsibilities for the planning, supervision, and implementation of the polycultural curriculum
    d.  A well-defined job description (loosely defined job descriptions can be a source of frustration for the coordinator and confusion for others with whom the coordinator must work)
    e.  A job title with teeth
    f.  Adequate budget

The major function of the coordinator is to engineer the programatic design for the polycultural curriculum. While the tasks for implementation will be shared with others in the organization, the coordinator's function is to synthesize all contributions into the "road map." The road map should delineate all roles—administrators, supervisors, consultants, and teachers. It should define committee action (Who? When? How? How often?). Behavioral questions such as these imply the necessity for behavioral-oriented criteria for assessing a polycultural curriculum. Without criteria, and statements of end products, there can be little meaningful assessment of the programs. The objectives of the organization must be stated in language that describes the behaviors of the learner. Such behavioral language can help the organization to analyze the effectiveness of the curriculum.

## 4.   A Timetable for Implementation

## 5.   A Budget Provided with Local Organizational Funds

The polycultural curriculum, to be successful, must have adequate financial resources for continuity. Effective programs cannot be properly designed where funding is tenuous and inadequate. Of the three commitments (verbal, written, and financial) budget speaks the loudest!

## 6. *Program Validation by the Ethnocultural Clientele Served*

The efficacy of the test for polycultural programs is its support and acceptance by the ethnocultural clientele served. Educational institutions are frequently criticized for poorly-implemented ethnocultural programs. Some critics assert these programs are not scholarly and do not measure up to the academic standards demanded of other subject-area disciplines. Other critics assert the ineffectiveness of such programs. Such charges, however valid they may seem, cannot be substantiated without a clear statement of behavioral criteria. Where there exists no such statement there is little the organization can claim, either as success or failure.

Ethnocultural groups are demanding greater participation in matters surrounding the operation of educational organizations. Their demands include the way polycultural programs are conceptualized, the way they are designed, the manner in which educators implement them, as well as salaries and other rewards. At the heart of these controversies lies a fundamentally unresolved issue: the evaluation of the educator's performance. One orderly resolution of this dilemma lies in the establishment of educational objectives for the organization and the delineation of them so that learner-behaviors can be demonstrated.

A well-implemented program for Chicano students could be assessed in terms of demonstrated needs being met in areas of bilingual/bicultural education. A relevant polycultural curriculum for Native American students could be assessed in terms of a declining drop-out rate, increased academic achievement and graduation. A report by the National Study of American Indian Education concluded that with few exceptions, the curriculum provided Native Americans in educational institutions is the same curriculum provided to other students. This, according to the report, is due to the influence of state curriculum guidelines, uniform teacher-education procedures, standardized texts, certification regulations, and prevailing teaching trends in the education of minorities. The false, underlying assumption is that the needs of all oppressed minorities are the same as the majority. Native Americans have persisted in holding on to their own traditions despite the poverty of many on reservations and in the cities.

Native American leaders assert that the curricula purported in public educational institutions reject and ignore the heritage of the Native American. And despite the availability of commercial materials, most elementary grade-level students experience a curriculum ignoring the past of Native Americans. A program that mentions Native Americans only at Thanksgiving has one message: in order to succeed in the system, Native Americans must denounce their identity, pride, and self-determination.

Polycultural curricula directed to meeting the needs of Native Americans should lay heavy emphasis on the history and culture of Native Americans—according to Native American educators. Such curricula should help all students and faculty deal with the racial stereotypes relating to Native Americans. The materials might focus on the multiplicity of tribal cultures. Parents and lay citizens should be involved in the development of such materials so that there is support from the Native American communities of the students, and clientele served. Finally, the National Study of American Indian Education advises that educational institutions must recognize the responsibility of Native Americans to define what is or is not good for Native Americans.

Educational institutions can anticipate continuing criticism from racial, ethnic, and cultural groups. "The schools are failing to meet the needs of our children!" will be the cry for some time to come. And who is to say this charge and others are false? We believe the institutional response to these charges lies in the establishment of behavioral objectives by educational organizations. When the outcomes of the organization are stated in a behavioral language that is understood by the student, the teacher, the parent, and lay citizen, all can determine together whether educational institutions have accomplished the stated goals.

## 7. *Program Accountability*

An accountability component should be included in any well-organized polycultural program. It is important that each unit of the curriculum achieve the capacity to evaluate pupil performance and staff effectiveness by performance criteria. Fundamentally, this means a sharing of power by educational institutions with community ethnocultural groups.

The critical importance of the philosophy statement can never be overemphasized. We have had the Emancipation Proclamation and the Declaration of Independence for a long time. Twenty years have gone by since the birth of the civil rights movement. Almost thirty years have elapsed since the United Nations proclaimed its objective of promoting human rights for all. But the violation of individual rights nationally and internationally has escalated—slavery and apartheid in South Africa and Rhodesia, massacres in Bangladesh, mass executions in Chile, suppression of political dissent in nations ruled by dictatorships, and racism in America. History has shown how violations of human freedom in one country are repeated in another. Slavery quickly became an international institution. The cycle of racism appears to be self-perpetuating. These inhumanities will continue until educators, students, parents, and lay citizens—nationally and internationally—speak out and act to prevent all manifestations of dehumanization. In American education we can begin to act through the implementation of more programs designed to promote better human understanding. A beginning step would be the implementation of a polycultural curriculum.

# IN-SERVICE EDUCATION: PLANNING AND IMPLEMENTING

> Multicultural skills are indispensable. If, that is, we are to
> understand each other clearly in this marvelously pluralistic land.[8]

Polycultural Education, from an in-service education perspective, should be viewed as both process and product. The in-service education workshop should be a professional growth process for the participants. At the same time, the workshop as a process, should be directed toward achieving a specific end product, a polycultural curriculum.

The in-service education workshop should be the facilitating mechanism for development of a network of personnel with polycultural skills. A network of highly skilled persons within an organization can provide the necessary leadership and technical assistance to other colleagues in developing, using, and assessing polycultural learning materials.

Five organizational stages should underscore planning for the in-service education workshop:

Stage 1: Deciding the details for implementing the workshop.
Stage 2: Communicating to workshop participants.
Stage 3: Implementing the workshop.
Stage 4: Evaluating the workshop.
Stage 5: Following-up the workshop.

## Stage 1: Deciding the Details

Once the decision is made by the organization to implement the workshop, a workshop planning committee should be organized. The planning committee should develop from needs assessment data, the goals and objectives for the workshop.

---

[8]Novak, Michael. "Was It A Case of Southern Chauvinism? *Minneapolis Star,* November 24, 1976.

An example of a workshop goal statement:

> The goal for the workshop is to provide skills in developing and assessing polycultural learning materials.

An example of statement of objectives to accomplish the goal:

1. 50 teachers and 50 administrators will be selected, one from each of the elementary and secondary schools.
2. The workshop participants will examine learning materials for racist, sexist, religious, and regional stereotypes, distortions, and untruths.
3. Participants will apply the organization's polycultural policy and criteria to the selected learning materials that are believed to be biased.
4. Participants will develop skills in modifying learning materials so that these materials are not biased.

A clear delineation of workshop goals and objectives should provide good direction for developing the workshop design. By workshop design we mean the sequence of activities by timetable that is expected to occur, from the opening of the workshop to its closing. Workshop designs may be modified into a number of formats depending upon the number of participants, the logistics of moving from large-group discussions to small groups, the length of time the workshop is to be implemented (e.g., seven hours or two days), the availability of resource consultants before and after the workshops, and the site of the workshop.

Two designs are basic to most workshops. They are the Consultant-Centered Model and the Participant-Centered Model.

## Consultant-Centered Model

The Consultant-Centered Model is highly structured but allows little opportunity for the workshop participants to do problem-solving activities. It is an excellent model where information-giving by resource consultant specialists is the desired goal. Many resource consultants prefer this model since the resource consultant can fulfill a commitment with a presentation to a large group, answer a few questions, collect the honorarium, and be off to another workshop in some other city. This is the least desirable way to utilize the services of the resource consultant. Resource consultants should be contracted to provide resource consultative assistance in the preplanning of the activities for a workshop, provide on-site assistance throughout the workshop, and, at a minimum, be advisor for a post-workshop briefing with the workshop planning staff. Keep in mind, however, caution in using the resource consultant in the Consultant-Centered workshop: be sure the contract for services includes the delivery of a prepared written statement or remarks to be presented by the consultant. This statement should be provided for the workshop planning committee well in advance of the workshop. Permission should be secured from the consultant to publish the statement or remarks in any subsequent publications of the workshop proceedings.

The Consultant-Centered Model is based on a presentation by the resource consultant. The presentations are usually made before a large group. The presentation is usually followed by a question-and-answer exchange with the participant audience. The large group is then subdivided into smaller discussion groups where the issues presented by the resource consultant are further clarified. Resource consultants should be invited to be active participants in these small-group discussions.

An example of a Consultant-Centered Model:

| | | |
|---|---|---|
| 1st Hour | A. | Welcome |
| | B. | Purposes for the workshop detailed |
| | C. | Charge to the participants |
| | D. | Introduction of the consultant speaker |
| 2nd Hour | Presentation by consultant | |
| 3rd Hour | Large-group interaction with consultant (question-answer exchange) | |
| 4th Hour | Small-group discussions (explore in further detail remarks by consultant) | |
| 5th Hour | Large-group discussion | |
| 6th Hour | Wrap-up summary statement | |

### Participant-Centered Model

The Participant-Centered Model offers more flexibility for participant problem-solving activities. While this model offers great potential for promoting aspects of team-building, there are some liabilities and limitations that planning staffs should be aware of.

One of the problems is in the psychology of human interaction. Participant-Centered workshops seem to foster participant expectations of group consensus decision-making. Problem-solving activities can sometimes be delayed where groups encounter difficulties moving to closure on some decisions. Task-oriented workshop participants sometimes experience high levels of frustration in Participant-Centered workshops. This is because these individuals come to the workshop with the expectation of getting on with the tasks. The group consensus advocates argue the merits of group ownership in every decision and group consensus before the movement by the group from one problem-solving activity to the next.

Both the Consultant-Centered and the Participant-Centered Models have great strengths and glaring weaknesses, and, therefore, the utility of one model over the other is not the issue here. The important consideration in the selection of a workshop model should be that of meeting the needs of the participants, particularly as these relate to the goals and objectives of the organization. We would suggest the following design for a workshop to address the application of polycultural criteria to selected learning materials:

| *Activity* | *Time Allocation* |
|---|---|
| I. Workshop participants get acquainted. | 5 Minutes |
| II. Workshop moderator summarizes for the participants the organization's philosophy, policy, and criteria regarding polycultural education. All the materials to be summarized by the workshop moderator should be in the folders provided for each participant well in advance of the workshop. | 20 Minutes |
| III. The large group may than be subdivided. Each of the smaller groups should then be assigned selected learning materials against which the participants are asked to apply the organization's philosophy, policy, and criteria regarding polycultural learning materials. | 4 Hours |

The selected learning materials may be from textbooks, news articles, editorials, brochures, pamphlets, or magazines/journals.

## Suggested Strategies:

### a.   Racism and Sexism in Learning Materials

An excellent document to have participants study is *A Time for Courage: The Story of the Declaration of Independence* by Esmond Wright. The participants might be asked to read the book through first and then apply the organization's philosophy, policy, and criteria to the material in the book. The participants should be asked to write down specific points showing whether the materials under study met or failed to meet the specified criteria.

In examining *A Time for Courage,* participants should do the following:

1. Examine the nationalistic imagery.
2. Note the elimination of first or last names for some of the characters in the story.
3. Assess whether the characters are treated equitably and whether the characters are treated as persons or objects.
4. Note the ethnocultural values projected:
   i.   Competition: Is it a Native American value?
   ii.  Do the children who are prejudiced learn what's wrong with being prejudiced?
   iii. Does the boy who says "I hate to waste my breath on a girl—especially an Indian" learn what is wrong with the racism and sexism of that statement?
   iv.  Does the story present any positive aspects of Native Americans?

### b.   Racism and Regional Chauvinism in Learning Materials

Ask the participants to read through the following paragraphs pointing out (using the organization's philosophy, policy, and criteria) examples of racial, religious, and regional chauvinism. Then have participants discuss reasons why these quotes should or should not be used in classroom teaching and learning activities:

> One of the strongest manifestations of the new ethnicity in American life is the support the solid South gave Jimmy Carter November 2. The South is still conservative, a Reagan advisor recently said, 'but blood ran thicker than ideology' this year. The South went Democratic in 1976 for ethnic reasons.
> Tom Wicker, the esteemed columnist, stresses the connection between himself and Jimmy Carter: "I can detect in Jimmy Carter

what I long ago recognized in myself—an indelible class sense, ingrained in us while growing up in the South during the Depression and fundamentally unaltered by later affluence."[9]

The question, 'Who is Jimmy Carter?' is a complex one that was partly answered by the voters November 2. The question, 'Who are southern Baptists?' is an even more complex one that now requires a special, if necessarily partial answer in the context, recent goings-on at the Baptist Church of Plains, Georgia.

The incident at Plains has been at least partly racial no matter that blacks have attended services at the church for years. No matter that the person primarily involved is not a Baptist. No matter that he is not a resident of the community.

As racism and race prejudice are prominent features in America's body politic, so they are besetting sins in the life of American churches in general and of Baptist churches in the South in particular. Racism is evil: it is nevertheless endemic in America.

It is endemic in the North as well as the South, in urban Detroit as well as rural Georgia, in the obscenities of Earl Butz as well as the obscenities of Lester Maddox and in the silk-stocking high churches as well as the blue-overalls low churches.

It may be remembered, moreover, that Southern Baptist Deacon Jimmy Carter would not be President-elect if it had not been for the overwhelming support of his black Baptist brothers and sisters.[10]

## c. *Religion and the Separation of Church and State*

Have the workshop participants examine program design samples of school-sponsored holiday assembly dramas or musical concerts. Ask the participants to assess the musical selections, scripts, and readings against the following principles:

1. A school may sponsor the study about religion but may not sponsor the practice of religion.
2. A school may expose students to all religious views but may not impose any particular view.
3. A school's approach to religions is one of instruction, not one of indoctrination.
4. A school should study what all people believe but not to teach a student what to believe.
5. A school's approach to religions is academic, not devotional.

---

[9]*Novak.*

[10]Valentine, Foy. "Perspective on Southern Baptists." *Minneapolis Tribune,* November 24, 1976.

The suggested examples cited are but a few of the many ways for applying criteria against selected learning materials. Organizations committed to polycultural efforts can insure the effective assessment and monitoring of such learning materials through a well-conceived set of criteria and a skilled staff.

It should be noted that there are educators who question the wisdom of establishing criteria for polycultural learning materials. They are the educators who accept without question their responsibilities for developing and using content criteria, but who are the first to feel imposed upon when asked to take steps in seeing that learning materials are nonracist, nonsexist, nonreligious, and nonregional. We would argue the position that organizations should establish a uniform set of criteria, i.e., content and polycultural combined in one instrument, and that all professionals in the organization receive in-service training in the application of that criteria to all learning materials.

Sometimes professional educators engage in unnecessary intellectualizing as a way of avoiding controversal issues. One national consultant advocated the coloring book as a medium for introducing certain historical aspects of Native American culture to Native American children. A traditionalist-oriented art consultant argued against using coloring books on the principle that such books violated basic principles of the discipline. Both were speaking from ethnocultural perspectives. The proponent for the use of coloring books was a Native American, the opponent was a non-Native American.

Who is to say which of the two positions is more valid? One thing is clear: controversies such as these substantiate our contention that well-defined criteria are needed to facilitate the elimination of racism, sexism, stereotypes, religious prejudice, and regional chauvinism from all learning materials.

## Stage 2: Communicating to Workshop Participants

This step may be accomplished by distributing two letters. The first, a general letter of invitation; the second, an informative letter giving more specific details of the workshop. The initial letter of invitation to potential participants should set forth information, such as the date for the workshop, the time, the place, and other pertinent facts. This letter should be mailed to participants well in advance of the workshop to permit participants to clear their calendars in advance of the scheduled workshop date.

The second letter should be sent to each participant just before the workshop date. Specific details should be provided, such as the general objectives to be accomplished, activities in which the participants are to be involved, and the amount of the stipends to be paid to the participants. A reply sheet should be provided with a stamped, self-addressed envelope.

The general letter to participants might be drafted like this:

> Dear _____:
>
> The purpose of the Polycultural Workshop is to help you, the participant, broaden your skills in the development, implementation, and evaluation of polycultural curriculum materials.
>
> To assist us in carrying out the workshop on (month, day, year), a National Resource Consultant, (name of consultant), will join us.
>
> You have been invited to attend this workshop because of your expressed interest in polycultural education. Your participation will help speed your school toward its goal of implementing a polycultural curriculum.
>
> The workshop will be at (address). The hours are from 9:00 a.m. to 4:00 p.m. You will be paid a stipend of (dollars).
>
> Please complete the enclosed form and return it to me at your earliest convenience.
>
> We hope to see you at the workshop!
>
> Very truly yours,
>
> John Doe, Coordinator
> Polycultural Education

## Stage 3: Implementing the Workshop

The success of the workshop will be related to the careful attention given to planning, the enthusiasm of the convener, and the choice of who helps facilitate the endeavor. By careful attention to planning, we mean checking out the workshop tasks to be accomplished, checking out the transportation and lodging for the guest consultant, and checking out the workshop facility for such things as lighting, seating arrangements, public address system, chalkboard, poster paper, masking tape, overhead projector and screen, lunch provisions, and other accommodations.

The coordinating workshop convener should brief the workshop facilitating staff to be sure everything is organized according to the planning schedule. Lay citizens and parents from ethnocultural groups should be invited to the workshops as observers. These persons could be vital resources in reinforcing the efforts of the organization.

## Stage 4: Evaluating the Workshop

The workshop should be evaluated in terms of its usefulness. In the final analysis, this can be answered only by each workshop participant. An evaluation design should be an outgrowth of suggestions from the participants. Some leading questions that should be addressed in the evaluation design are:

- Was the workshop beneficial to you?
- Do you feel you have been provided new information or new insights?
- Do you feel more skilled in the development of polycultural materials?
- Are you more familiar with commercially available learning materials?
- Do you feel more competent in the use of polycultural materials?
- Did you find the resource consultants helpful?
- In what ways did you find the consultants helpful?

Evaluations written by participants do not always tell the complete success or failure story for the workshop. There are times when it may appear that these evaluations are at odds with the personal observations of the workshop process. Sometimes discussions with the participants bring forth unexpected comments, some positive and some negative. Here the rule of thumb is the axiom, Consider the source. Off-the-cuff comments of participants should not be ignored. In the workshop evaluation instrument there should be a section where participants may register comments about the workshop. Doubtless many people simply do not like to say negative things, even on an anonymous questionnaire, so it is possible that the ratings will be more positive than negative. On the other hand, there is some evidence in the research literature that suggests vocal critics are not often representative of the total group. The workshop planning-evaluation committee should take positive satisfaction and pride in the organization that sponsors and supports a workshop on polycultural education. In such a case, the message of commitment is much more important than the medium.

## *Stage 5: Following-Up the Workshop*

The working criteria developed and used by the workshop participants should be later synthesized into a formal instrument for classroom teacher use. Clearly stated suggestions for using the criteria should be interwoven into the instrument. The polycultural programs coordinator may find it helpful to convene the *ad hoc* writing committee to revise and refine the criteria from time to time. The *ad hoc* writing committee can accomplish this task through materials-testing sessions in which curriculum materials are tested against the newly developed working criteria.

In summary the organization's philosophy, policy, and learning materials criteria will be as effective as the people using them. Follow-up is an ongoing, never-ending process but the payoffs for skilled and competent staff are immeasurable.

# FINANCING POLYCULTURAL PROGRAMS

Any program design for polycultural education should evolve from a comprehensive organizational assessment of student needs. The organization should then allocate adequate budget to implement the program. While this is the ideal way to implement educational programs, it is far from the reality of too many educational organizations. It is unfortunate that many organizations set the budgets first, and then attempt piecemeal efforts at program planning for the students. This practice of "cart-horse" administration, along with dwindling fiscal resources, all but negate any chance for a nationwide thrust at eliminating ethnocultural illiteracy. It is unfortunate that as a nation, we spend billions of dollars annually to study our distant celestial neighbor the moon, but we seem unwilling to finance programs that would help us learn about the neighbors of this planet.

The psychology of reversed priorities underscores too many federal-level and state-level attempts at multicultural education. Few if any of the legislative programs, or the multiplicity of federal and state laws, provide the funding necessary to uproot from American life the vestiges of racism, sexism, religious discrimination, regional chauvinism, and all the other ethnocultural manifestations of dehumanization.

There are three organizational expressions of commitment to programs for polycultural education: the verbal pronouncement by officials in the organization, written statements of policy, and the budget. While the importance of verbal and written expressions in climate setting within organizations is great, it is the allocation of dollars that transmits the stronger signal.

Sometimes verbal expressions of commitment by organization officials are politically motivated. Some officials make false promises in the heat of confrontation with ethnocultural pressure groups. In educational politics, it is best to press for a straightforward update on the organization's position with regard to polycultural education. Beware of the tendencies of some organizations to produce sophisticated publications detailing in "Madison Avenue" fashion their commitments to polycultural education. Too many brochures hypocritically proclaim the organization's dedication to equal opportunity and affirmative action.

The two test questions which will either prove or disprove the issue of commitment are the following:

- Where is the budget to implement the polycultural program?
- Who controls the budget?

The budget for implementing the polycultural program should be under the control of the administrator of the program. A major fiscal responsibility of the coordinator is to prepare a budget to carry out the goals and objectives for the program. The coordinator should be knowledgeable and skilled in budget-development. This must include a thorough understanding of every component in the budget.

The funding sources for polycultural programs sometimes suggest the organization's commitment. A budget provided by the local organization is a positive expression of commitment. But the absence of locally provided budget and/or the total dependence on outside funding, suggests a lack of commitment by that organization to polycultural educational programs. Further, the total dependence of the organization on outside funding suggests that the polycultural educational endeavors are to be kept isolated and disconnected from the regular curriculum.

All budgetary requests to fund polycultural programs should be submitted to funding organizations with a proposal for a grant. This is the polycultural program coordinator's most critical fiscal responsibility. This is because program development and the ability to win grants often determine the success or failure of organizations seeking funding.

Several proposal-development stages deserve special attention by the coordinator:

1. Statement of the problem and the needs
2. Statement of the general goals and objectives
3. Statement delineating an historical perspective of the organization

4. Statement delineating the program components in terms of specific behavioral objectives
5. Statement mapping the timetable for the implementation of the program
6. Statement of needed budget
7. Proposal negotiations and the politics of grant-winning
8. Statement explaining staff responsibilities.

## 1.   Statement of the Problem and the Needs

The first step in proposal development is to identify the problems and translate them into needs. Begin with an assessment of student needs. The report of your findings might show a correlation between diverse racial-ethnic-cultural populations in a school and the increase of conflict among the various groups. This assessment might show the need for a polycultural curriculum as a vehicle for minimizing racial-ethnic-cultural conflicts. The report might show the disruptive influences of racial-ethnic-cultural conflicts on the school organization and the cumulative effects on patterns of student achievement. The assessment might show the impact of negative racist attitudes of teachers and students, and how these affect behaviors that create disequilibrium within the school organization. The needs may then be substantiated in the proposal with the necessary supportive data, such as the number of conflicts racially motivated, declining student achievement, increasing faculty turnover, low staff morale, increasing parent dissatisfaction, etc.

## 2.   Statement of the General Goals and Objectives

The second step is the statement of goals. Remember that your general goal is to establish the polycultural curriculum. But specific objectives must be stated in straightforward, behavioral language. For example:

> During the implementation of this program, we will see a definite decrease in the number of racial-ethnic-cultural conflicts in verbal exchanges between students using racial-ethnic-cultural stereotypes.

Once the objective has been delineated, the activity for carrying out the objective must be stated. For example:

> Program content for the polycultural curriculum for grades $\underline{X}$

through Y̱ will focus on dispelling racist myths and stereotypes for A̱ and Ḇ racial-ethnic-cultural groups.

A statement of evaluation should follow each statement of objective and accompanying activities. For example:

Records of conflict-incidents will be maintained by each classroom teacher. Curricula materials dispelling racist myths and stereotypes will be developed and field-tested against criteria established by the organization.

## 3. Statement Delineating an Historical Perspective of the Organization

The third step of the proposal should denote general background information leading to the statement of the problem and the need for a polycultural curriculum. This should be done in narrative fashion. Any written documentation affirming the organization's commitment to polycultural education should be interwoven with the historical background.

## 4. Statement Delineating the Program Components in Terms of Specific Behavioral Objectives

In the fourth step, be sure to detail each component of the proposed curriculum. Again, state this in straightforward, behavioral language: who is responsible for doing what. A description of each of the program components will identify the schools actively implementing the polycultural program, the number of students to be served in the program, the kinds of program designs for grade-age-interest level student-groupings and for what periods of time.

## 5. Statement Mapping the Timetable for the Implementation of the Program

The fifth step of the proposal will set forth the timetables for implementing the program. The coordinator must maintain a clear focus on the time schedule of the polycultural curriculum if it is to run smoothly. A timetable should list on a single page all major implementation tasks, their starting dates, and their completion dates. Major implementation tasks should include the requisition and distribution of equipment and supplies, screening and selection of staff, planning and providing in-service education to staff, selection of student participants, planning and preparing of curricula materials, organizing and scheduling activities for the *ad hoc* writing committee, and perhaps most important, the screening and selection of the program coordinator.

## 6.   *Statement of Needed Budget*

The sixth step of the proposal should be a detailed budget showing the number of dollars requested for the administration and evaluation of a polycultural curriculum. This should include: professional personnel salaries, clerical salaries, instructional equipment, telephones, mileage costs, special curricula materials, research materials, housing space and maintenance, pre-service education workshops for staff, in-service education workshops for staff, instructional hardware, instructional software, and salaries for parent, student, and citizen participation. A statement of justification and rationale should accompany each expenditure category.

## 7.   *Proposal Negotiations and the Politics of Grants-Winning*

It is unfortunate that some polycultural proposals for grants are rejected on the basis of political considerations, while many poorly conceived and poorly written proposals are funded on the basis of sheer expertise in grants-winning. One organization in a major urban city reported submitting a comprehensive proposal for the development of multiracial curricula materials. The proposal was rejected by a higher echelon, state-level official. It seems the organization had denied the official's request for a more comprehensive written statement of commitment by the organization to school desegregation.

A proposal for a pilot bussing exchange program between a central city school system and suburban school districts was funded despite the submission of a piecemeal proposal. The reason? Metropolitan exchange bussing program proposals were regarded, at that time, as sure bets for funding. In another situation, a private foundation agreed to funding a proposal for a grant before it was ever written.

Two general guidelines should direct the organization's development of the proposal for a grant. First, a funded proposal is a proposal whose political and ideological time has come. Second, nonfunded proposals should not be discarded! Instead, these should be filed away for future reference, redevelopment, and submission at a more propitious time.

A key consideration for securing proposal funding from public and private agencies is the skill of winning grants. There is a multiplicity of strategies followed by organizations to secure funding—from the design and development of the proposal to negotiating it. Those who are charged with these responsibilities must be permitted mobility and flexibility in their role positions. This is because the skill of winning grant proposals requires, in addition to writing skills, selling skills, and lobbyist skills, a working knowledge of legislation, national programs, regulations and policies at the federal, state, and local levels. These capabilities should be considered when selecting the coordinator for polycultural programs.

Grants-winning skills must be developed through personal, one-to-one communications. The political support necessary to influence the funding of proposals can be facilitated in social conversations, a personal visit with a key official of the funding agency, a cup of coffee and conversation with a legislator, a personal note of interest to the chairperson of the proposal reader's committee.

One author of a polycultural proposal was called for an immediate conference with the official of a funding agency. It was the day before the funding agency was to make decisions on several proposals submitted. The official was upset that three proposals had been submitted from the same organization. Two of the three proposals had identical narrative descriptions, page by page, but carried different project titles and budgets. Informal conversations with the state official brought both coordinator and the state official to the realization that the identical pages in the two proposals were due to a collating error in the office of the funding agency. The pages were quickly changed to the appropriate proposals and made ready for the decision-making committee.

## 8. *Statement Explaining Staff Responsibilities*

The eighth step, proposal development and proposal implementation, should be shared by the organizational proposal-writing team.

The coordinator can facilitate the team process by preparing a "Proposal Preparation Functions Chart." This chart should detail the tasks to be accomplished in developing the proposal. The chart should enumerate the persons responsible for contributing the information, such as the date and timetables for accomplishing the tasks, and the process for eliciting feedback from the team. The feedback process should provide the coordinator valuable information on the attitudes, problems, and concerns of the team members. Cumulative feedback data from team members can be used by the coordinator as a basis for decision-making.

Once the "Proposal Preparation Functions Chart" has been prepared by the coordinator, copies should be provided to all members of the organization, and a team briefing should be scheduled. The briefing should focus on the tasks of team members. At the briefing, the coordinator should lay heavy emphasis on questions from team members. These should be discussed in candor so that team members understand their responsibilities for the development of the proposal.

Proposal development and implementation sometimes break down at critical stages because team members are unclear on the nature of their responsibilities. A "Proposal Preparation Functions Chart" should be prepared. Such a chart should facilitate staff understanding of the mission so that the proverbial "right hand knows what the left hand is doing."

The preparation of a budget and the proposal for a grant should both be predicated upon the procuring of better services for the ethnocultural student populations served. The budget and the proposal for grant can insure a fiscal base, and with it the stabilization and continuity necessary for the polycultural program to be a success. Helping students become culturally literate and helping them to broaden their national and international cultural perspectives should be the concomitant educational imperative!

# COMMUNITY INVOLVEMENT
# IN POLYCULTURAL EDUCATION

Community involvement is a collaborative process involving parents, students, educators, and lay citizens working together to achieve mutually desired goals. Ethnocultural community groups can render invaluable assistance to organizations implementing polycultural programs. Ethnocultural community organizations can serve the educational institutions in a number of ways: providing counsel on the concerns of ethnocultural groups, acting as sounding boards to the organization, acting as communications links between the school organizations and the community, functioning as community monitors for supportive community activities, and providing a supportive voice to the school organization.

Functions such as these can be carried out by a Polycultural Community Advisory Committee organized and coordinated by the school system. Several considerations should be regarded as guiding principles for establishing such an advisory committee.

The first consideration should be membership. Membership should reflect the racial, ethnic, and cultural diversity of the student populations served. Representatives from other racial-ethnic-cultural organizations should be available to give support to the committee. These members should not be expected to speak for their racial, ethnic, or cultural organization, but rather to serve as liaison between their organization and the school organization.

Voting membership should be reserved on the advisory committee so that a proportion of nonmember lay citizens are permitted to attend any meeting of the committee and enjoy full voting privileges.

What about the meeting itself? Community organizations should take turns hosting the Polycultural Community Advisory Committee. Meeting at the headquarters of various ethnocultural community organizations can provide the members firsthand opportunities to experience diverse ethnocultural settings. An ethnic dinner meeting almost always assures a good turnout. Committee members will find it hard to resist an evening of *burritos, Wiener schnitzel,* or black-eyed peas and collard greens.

The committee should meet regularly as long as there is a need felt by committee members. All meetings should be open to the public and scheduled at different hours and on different days to encourage maximum participation.

A diverse range of educational topics should be the basis for committee planning:

1. Improving the curriculum
2. Assisting in the development and implementation of in-service education programs
3. Hosting information-sharing forums on local educational issues
4. Serving as classroom resource volunteers
5. Serving as local community hosts for visiting guest consultants
6. Serving as coordinating agency for annual school-community intercultural events.

The undergirding philosophy for establishing ethnocultural advisory committees should be an abiding respect for the cultural norms of all ethnocultural groups. This means scheduling meeting dates so that these do not violate the religious holidays of committee members. It means respecting the determination of oppressed minority groups to have a greater voice in educational decisions affecting their children. Educators sometimes commit the error of underestimating this determination.

A community advisory committee of a major city found that through cohesiveness and persistence it could influence the decisions made within the school system. This committee was effective in helping the school organization secure a sizeable federal grant that brought needed services to children and new employment opportunities to a number of lay citizens. Once the program became operational, the advisory committee shifted its focus to monitoring the programmatic and fiscal aspects of the program. Committee members visited schools to see the services provided through the grant. Conversations between committee members and students led committee members to expand the committee's membership to include students. Committee members then began requesting more information on the budget, sometimes raising questions on what they felt to be unwise expenditures. This committee became more than an advisory body. It became symbolic of what community involvement should be! Its productivity gave credence to the notion that community involvement breeds increasing levels of community awareness. It was interesting to note that after a year of activity, the committee found itself identifying new areas for input. It then set about redefining and expanding its objectives. That is community involvement!

Members of community advisory committees, through active involvement with school organizations, sometimes develop new levels of understanding regarding the goals of the school organizations. A community advisory committee in one city directed the following questions to a school organization official:

- "Does the curriculum meet the needs of blacks, Native Americans, and Chicanos?"
- "How is your work with curriculum development related to human relations?" .
- "What curriculum procedures could be instituted to better meet the needs of all segments of society?"
- "How can you justify equal support to the ethnic studies program and to groups opposed to desegregation?"
- "Is there evidence that ethnic study mitigates racism?"
- "I am concerned with world citizenship more than with ethnic identifications, and why haven't we gone beyond these narrow boundaries?"

The school organization's official person fielded the questions in straightforward candor. A letter of appreciation from the committee underscored the importance of his candor in communicating with the committee:

Dear _____:

Frankly I was amazed to receive your written presentations—because you used it and departed from it so naturally that it all seemed spontaneous. We learned a tremendous amount from you. Monday's minutes turned out to be the longest we've ever had. The committee members' questions seemed excellent, which means that you elicited their interest. I'm sure that we'll be asking you for information again. Thank you for your excellent response to this request!

Community involvement can be a growth experience for both the school organization and the ethnocultural community organizations. Community involvement is a positive phenomenon if it facilitates the delivery of services to meet the needs of students. But educators, parents, and lay citizens should be cognizant of potentially negative influences from some cause groups and their negative impact on the educational process.

School boards and school administrations are witness to the increasing effort of well-organized, sociopolitical cause groups to change various aspects of education—teaching and learning methodology, media, administrative organization, and decision making. These efforts may or may not produce improved learning conditions for the prime focus of education: children. This is because school systems and school communities are still engaged in the process of defining what ought to comprise education.

The challenge for educators is to communicate with the diverse ethnocultural organizations and ethnocultural groups so that the process of defining what education ought to be is a collaborative effort of school and community. Our failure to do this as educators can only escalate the negative forces of cause groups. Cause groups have learned from the early vanguard of black civil rights groups, Chicano activists, and Native American movements. Now it is the ecologists, the integrationists, the segregationists, the phylogenetic separatists, the gray panthers, the feminists, and the gay liberationists—all with important messages. Public education is often the arena where the philosophies of such groups are juxtaposed. School board meetings are becoming ethnocultural arenas where board members and school administrations find themselves gladiators pitted against militant cause groups. These juxtaposed ideologies present a potential for polycultural conflict—conflict many times for the better of education and many times for the worse.

Some cause groups present glaring contradictions between their pronouncements as change agents and what they actually practice. Unfortunately for some of these groups, change is predicated on cause and effect—a specific action or actions on the part of the change agent and the effect that action has on the targets to be changed. But according to the behavioral sciences, lasting change occurs only when the individual internalizes a new set of values that gives rise to his or her attitudes and, ultimately, behaviors. The ecologists sometimes discuss air pollution, rapid transit systems, freeway transportation, and school desegregation as if these were all separate and unrelated to the increasing racial polarization. Some minority groups contend that the feminist movement has generally failed to address racism as it relates to the Native American female, the Chicano female, and the black female. Other minorities now contend that the lumping of cause groups together is a deliberate attempt to keep oppressed peoples divided among themselves and conquered.

Cause groups are prone to pronounce that their own position is to support coalitions of cause groups as long as they are committed to increasing opportunities for minorities and other oppressed groups. We are not supportive of such groups when the achievement of their goals and objectives insures the displacement of minorities and women in employment opportunities. Our rationale is based on the sad reality that the criteria for selection and placement of minorities in newly created job opportunities are what have historically excluded minorities: seniority and experience.

The would-be implementer of polycultural programs would do well to know the basic politics of cause groups. Cause groups employ a multiplicity of tactics as a means to achieve their ends. There is, however, a similarity underscoring the efforts they use to get the listening ear of school boards and school administrations. First, there is a cry for change at public board meetings. Then there is a demand for a private meeting with the chief school official, usually the superintendent, at which time a preliminary agenda is presented by the group. Usually there are two agendas—a suggested agenda and a subliminal one. The suggested agenda will usually address general social goals for change that few would argue with, for example, apple pie and Good Samaritanism. The subliminal agenda is usually a move to establish organizational inroads into the organization. Once established within the organization, these groups will commence carrying out their own objectives.

Unfortunately, cause groups too often seek refuge in already powerless, newly established organizations struggling for survival. The internal struggles for power within these organizations, and their limited resources, are sure to result in a diffusion of energies, frustration, and conflict, as well as the ultimate failure for the to-be-implemented polycultural program. Divide-and-conquer is a well known strategy that organizations already empowered within school organizations sometimes employ to insure the failure of the less powerful units.

If a cause-group proposal should merit consideration from the school board, the administrative staff committee should convene (1) representatives from the community, (2) representatives from the cause group making the proposal, and (3) community organizations and parents to review the proposal and to discuss the implications for the students whose lives will be affected by it. If the decision is to approve the proposal presented, processes and procedures for getting the program started should be set into motion. Clarification as to where the program is to reside, under whose supervision; reporting lines, goals and objectives, and budget provisions should be detailed with clarity so everyone can understand them. The political nature of cause groups mitigate against the institution of tenured role-positions. Instead, there should be annual assessment of achieved objectives and a periodic turnover of personnel in charge of cause-group programs to negate political entrenchments. Once commitment is made by the school organization to implement a proposal initiated by a cause group, job descriptions should be established and posted to insure opportunities for all interested staff and community. No direct appointments should be made by the organization on the basis of recommendations by the proposing cause groups. Interviews should be conducted according to the organization's personnel procedures.

The organization of cause groups is on the increase. School boards and school administrations must now address the question of how to be most effective in working with them to improve the delivery of services to the students whom the educational institutions serve.

Educators, students, parents, and lay citizens should avoid confusing the terms "community involvement," "community participation," and "community control." Although these terms are not mutually exclusive, and although they convey different meanings to different people, they are all interrelated. One may participate in the activities of a school organization without really becoming involved. Community control is a community's grip on the school's three P's: people, program, and power.

Another key matter to consider, as the issue of community involvement is examined, is the phenomenon of goals and expectations. One possible area of conflict might be the expectations of the Polycultural Community Advisory Committee and the objectives of the school organization. Educators, students, parents, and lay citizens must work to see that these are not at cross-purposes.

Finally, community involvement is necessary if polycultural education is ever to succeed in the eyes of community ethnocultural groups. We believe the key to achieving community involvement is accountability. Accountability can be built into the structure of the polycultural curriculum through clearly stated program objectives understood by all. The school-community network can then strive together to achieve the capacity for improving pupil performance and staff effectiveness. To develop better three-way accountability between parents, students, and teachers, several strategies are suggested for ethnocultural community organizations:

1. Sponsor discussion forums on the need for polycultural education
2. Become involved in the affairs of the school organization so that relevant issues and concerns are kept alive until addressed
3. Invite school-organization personnel to attend and participate with the community in addressing community-defined issues
4. Demand educational accountability through clearly defined organization standards and clearly stated criteria and procedures for evaluating the performance of students and educators.

A polycultural curriculum will be as strong as the community support it receives. That support should be cultivated by educators into a network of educators, students, parents, and lay citizens working together for the common goal: to help students broaden their national and international cultural perspectives. A community's most precious resource is its children and youth. They must be provided with every opportunity to grow, for that growth is the key to resolving the problems of air pollution, water pollution, and the most deadly of all pollutions—the pollution of racism!

# SO-CALLED LIBERALS AND
# SO-CALLED INTELLECTUALS

Organizational efforts to address manifestations of dehumanization have been effectively resisted, and in too many instances, completely stifled—not by the so-called racists, but by the so-called liberals and the so-called intellectuals. This chapter focuses on these types because they appear to be well understood in the circles of many professional educators.

Discussing these two types, liberals and intellectuals, serves a special purpose: to alert those who would initiate polycultural programs to these potential obstructionists. Contrary to the belief of some that colonized people seldom conquer (because they are always divided, fighting each other), colonized people do unite by communicating with one another. Our conversations with professional colleagues, from New York to California and from Michigan to Mississippi, substantiate our contention that the so-called liberals and the so-called intellectuals merit careful scrutiny by those who would implement polycultural programs.

Our perceptions of the so-called liberal and the so-called intellectual are not really new revelations. The late noted historian Dr. Carter G. Woodson offered an admonishment worth repeating to the oppressed ethnocultural groups of today:

> History shows that it does not matter who is in power or what revolutionary forces take over the government, those who have not learned to do for themselves and have to depend solely on others never obtain any more rights or privileges in the end than they had in the beginning.
> ... When the desired purposes of these so-called friendly groups will have been served, they will have no further use for the Negro and will drop him just as the Republican machine has done.[11]

When we translate Dr. Woodson's message into the civil rights

---

[11]Woodson, Carter G. *Mis-Education of the Negro.* Associated Publishers, 1933. pp. 186, 188.

movements or the struggle of colonized people today, we find striking parallels. The late Malcolm X warned of liberals and intellectuals wresting control of the civil rights movement from the hands of the people who suffered most. Both CORE (Congress of Racial Equality) and SNCC (Student Non-Violent Coordinating Committee) found it necessary, on more than one occasion, to dismiss from their organizational ranks certain liberals and intellectuals.

It should be noted here that when we refer to so-called liberals and so-called intellectuals, our reference is within the context of observable behaviors—what these types do and say that others perceive to be dehumanizing. It would be erroneous for the reader to assume from these observations that so-called liberals and so-called intellectuals are only found in certain ethnocultural groups. They can be found in every ethnocultural group, and have one thing in common: both types have special destructive potentials for negating polycultural efforts.

## So-Called Liberals

What then should the would-be implementers of polycultural programs be on the alert for? Those who would implement polycultural programs should be on the alert for "gaming" by so-called liberals and so-called intellectuals. This phenomenon is subtle, insidious, and very difficult to deal with. One example of gaming appears when a decision-making group is moving toward consensus. If the consensus is toward implementing a multicultural program, or a bussing program, or an affirmative action program (any program that might improve the *status quo* of oppressed ethnocultural groups), so-called liberals will invariably move to action. They will invariably proclaim their commitments to equal educational opportunity, but qualify this proclamation with a caution that perhaps the decision should be delayed until the housing issue is resolved. So-called liberals are fully aware that nine states to date have enacted legislation against the construction of low-income housing in suburban areas. Keen observers of recent racist literature relating to genetics and IQ will recall these materials were by-and-large authored by nationally-acclaimed liberal scholars from prestigious universities. It is unfortunate that too many of these racist studies are accepted as scholarly truths.

Carl Rowan provides a piercing analysis of a watered-down definition of equal opportunity by a person considered in many circles to be a liberal. The following article concerns former HEW secretary, Caspar W. Weinberger:

> Finally Weinberger gave his own declarations of the meaning of equal opportunity. He said it is the right to compete equally for the rewards of excellence, not share in its fruits regardless of personal effort.
>
> When taxes are high and prices higher, and jobs are scarce and hope is even harder to find, millions of Americans looking for an easy scapegoat will embrace Weinberger's litany.
>
> Blame-placing becomes an easy exercise. The affluent, who got that way through a hundred government fights of one kind or another, are apt to think that theirs are the rewards of excellence while all the other miserable clods are trying to sop up gravy without expending proper personal effort.[12]

Racism has still another subtle way of operating against oppressed ethnocultural groups through the well-known liberal ploy, divide-and-conquer. Time after time the so-called liberals in decision-making or decision-influencing roles have set into motion, sometimes by design, sometimes unwittingly, certain conditions that set one oppressed ethnocultural group against another. And while these already disenfranchised oppressed ethnocultural groups fought each other, the real purveyors of conflict (the so-called liberals) observed the action unchallenged. Dr. Carter G. Woodson prophetically pinpointed the issue:

> . . . too weak to overcome foes who have purposely taught negroes how to quarrel and fight about trifles until their enemy overcame them. This is the keynote to the control of the so-called inferior races by the self-styled superior. The one thinks and plans while the other in excited fashion seizes upon and destroys his brother with whom he should cooperate.[13]

From the two examples presented in this chapter, it would be erroneous to hypothesize an overly simplistic analysis of such complex behaviors by so-called liberals. It is safe to assume that the psychology of racism is at the roots of such behaviors, although

---

[12]Rowan, Carl. *Minneapolis Star,* July 28, 1975.
[13]*Woodson,* p. 1.

there is not empirical hard data to support this contention. There are, however, the perceptions of professional colleagues to substantiate this assumption of racism.

It is particularly distressing to find that many of these types are members of oppressed ethnocultural groups. James and Mary Norman Tillman, noted black social engineers, went a step further in examining the anthropological profiles of so-called liberals and so-called intellectuals:

> Black intellectuals and white liberals however defined and of whatever variety have played critical roles in shaping the race relations landscape of the United States. Because both groups have avowed their commitment to equal justice for blacks, their assumptions about goals, procedures and directions with rare exceptions, have gone unexamined. This condition if permitted to continue can become counter-productive.[14]

## So-Called Intellectuals

The would-be initiator of polycultural programs should be especially alert for the bahaviors of so-called intellectuals in group decision-making processes: listen for overly rhetorical oratory, watch for the "power plays," steer clear of the "rap" sessions without specific goal-accomplishment agendas.

Those who would initiate the implementation of polycultural programs should be keenly attuned to the game-playing skills of so-called intellectuals. Our belief is that the so-called intellectual has as a basic objective the desire to obscure major issues affecting the progress of oppressed ethnocultural groups and, in doing so, the desire to prolong any decision-making process that could facilitate the achievement of humanistic equity.

Those who administer polycultural programs should look beyond the definitions of "progress" for oppressed ethnocultural groups, as defined by the so-called intellectual. It is not surprising that after nearly three decades of marches and protests we find the plight of oppressed ethnocultural groups relatively unchanged. But the so-called intellectuals would be quick to point out the increase of minorities enrolled in colleges and universities around the na-

---

[14]Tillman, James, and Tillman, Mary Norman. "Black Intellectuals, White Liberals and Race Relations." *Phylon,* 1972.

tion. This data is used to support the distorted contention of some liberals and intellectuals that competence via educational preparation assures equitable upward mobility. But one has only to observe the sudden evacuation of decaying cities and the abandonment of debt-ridden school districts to understand the appearance on the scene of newly elected minority-group officials. And after the newly acquired offices are totaled up nationally, minority group representation is still proportionately less. The Tillmans provide a plausible explanation for this phenomenon:

> In general America promised the newly emancipated blacks that in proportion as they mastered one area of cultural competence she would reward them by permitting them to operate on a par with whites in those areas for which their previous mastery had prepared them. Consequently, blacks who mastered, as many did, the education motif came to believe that they would not suffer differential and unequal treatment in the areas of employment for which their education and training had prepared them. They soon discovered the folly of their believing this country's pronouncements about equality.[15]

These examples of behaviors by so-called liberals and so-called intellectuals were presented to bring to focus a message for those who would initiate polycultural programs. The message is this: develop a repertoire of coping strategies.

In developing a repertoire of coping strategies we would suggest the following:

1. Understand the reality of organizational politics. Changing the *status quo* in organizations toward the acceptance of polycultural programs will not be easy. This is because most people tend to choose what they have always had.
2. Plan thoroughly for the implementation of proposals for grants to implement polycultural programs.
3. Understand all the issues related to the initiation and administering of a polycultural program:
   a. Know the issue.
   b. Know the rationale behind the issue.
   c. Know the assumptions underscoring the rationale.
   d. Know all the forces for and against the issue under consideration.

---

[15]*Tillman and Tillman.*

4. Understand every component of a polycultural program:
   a. Know the goals and objectives to be accomplished.
   b. Know the role expectations and tasks to be performed by every participant to implement the program successfully.
   c. Know the exact timetables for accomplishing each of the tasks to be performed.
   d. Know the dollar-cost for every component in the program.
   e. Know how the success or failure of each component in the program will be measured, evaluated, and accounted for.

It is unfortunate that the omnipresence of racism and sexism in organizations necessitates the delineation of details for such a chapter as this. This book offers no apologies, for these details are realities certain to be faced by those who would implement polycultural programs. It is most unfortunate that the so-called liberals and so-called intellectuals contribute to the promulgation of these ugly realities. The so-called liberals and intellectuals, with all their capabilities and formal educations, are sadly in reality the miseducated. If educating America's most precious resource (its children and youth) to higher levels of ethnocultural literacy is ever to be a reality, then those who are concerned must move to action. Our children and youth deserve our best efforts and nothing less!

# A PLANETARY PERSPECTIVE

> The *Times* conducted an inquiry last week into rumors spreading through Washington that Mr. Nixon often used ethnic and religious epithets, that some of them showed up on White House tapes on Watergate matters, and that others had been edited from the White House transcripts of the tomes made available to the House Judiciary Committee . . . A number of former high-level White House aides said that, while Mr. Nixon frequently used ethnic and religious epithets in private, they generally were not meant seriously."[16]

America is in a period of escalating ethnocultural isolation. The catalyst for the concomitant conflicts and hostilities is the phenomenon of racism. This is the racism that threatens to colonize America's educationally cheated children into perpetuity.

What is a colony and who are the colonized? A colony is a community of segregated, isolated people whose life-styles and life chances are directed by economic and political influences outside the colony. Every major city harbors a colony. The absentee-owned farms of New England are colonies. The federally subsidized plantations of the South are colonies. The freeway-ringed, but suburban controlled, central cities are colonies. This twentieth century colonization is far more devastating than any territorial imperialism of the British, for this is a colonization of Americans by other Americans. The ethnocultural groups (all colonized people — the exploited blacks, the Native Americans, the migrant workers, and poor whites) are as effectively colonized as any nineteenth century British outpost.

The tragedy of this condition is that Americans have allowed a national climate of prejudice, hate, racism, and sexism to grow.

America's educational, social, political, religious, and economic institutions must begin responding collectively to stop this condition. Educational institutions can contribute to this collective effort through the implementation of polycultural programs. Failure to be constructively responsive can only lead to more racial, ethnic, and cultural hostilities.

---

[16]Hersh, Seymour M. "Racial Slurs Reportedly Made by Nixon." *Minneapolis Tribune,* May 12, 1974.

## Can America Choose Wisely Between Polycultural Curriculum and Polycultural Conflict?

There are three major barriers to polycultural education becoming a reality for educational institutions. We have labeled these as colonizers: institutional, structural, and human. Institutional colonizers are those societal systems whose essential framework, characteristics, and mechanisms deny the colonized access to power. Structural colonizers are the policies and practices derived from executive action of the institutions. These actions help maintain the equilibrium of colonizer-held power and thus the system of colonization. Human colonizers are the individuals whose actions or inactions create the network of structural policies now entrapping the people of the colony. Structural and human colonizers are products of a society polluted by racism. If institutional racism is a pollution, then it would seem to follow that the real polluters are those individuals behind the institutions.

Why is it that America permitted bigotry to evolve as a cultural norm? How could it be that an American president and a secretary of agriculture in the twentieth century could find a place for ethnic and religious epithets in their daily conversations? How could the accused (and their sympathizers) attempt to excuse such racist behaviors by rationalizing that other American presidents were known to have used rough, ethnic language in private conversation? What have social and educational institutions done, and what is being done to help American schoolchildren understand the dehumanizing nature of expressions such as wop, mackerel-snapper, broad, nigger, honkey, pollock, gook, jew boy, polak. There is a need for polycultural education for all Americans!

The need for polycultural education can be seen in the ugly, colonizing manifestations of racism in America. It can be seen in the retrenchment of school systems from desegregation. It can be seen in the absence of enthusiasm from federal, state, and local governmental institutions to change normative patterns of racist behaviors. There are still antidesegregation amendments in appropriation bills for federal aid to education, and antidesegregation clauses in federal guidelines. There are still barriers to open occupancy housing programs.

The need for polycultural education can be seen in the impact of political and educational decisions that are made from racist premises. The U.S. Department of Justice intervened in the Richmond desegregation case, suggesting that the Circuit Court of Appeals reverse, modify, or defer its desegregation order. The U.S. Justice Department intervened in the Detroit desegregation case, as a friend of the defendents, against desegregation. And a proposal by Senator Abraham Ribicoff, calling for the equity of sharing by all races in the desegregation process, was overwhelmingly defeated by the House of Representatives during the 92nd Congress.

No state at the time of this writing has established a desegregation enforcement agency with the power to insure local school district compliance. No state has advocated a statewide desegregation of the all-white, as well as the all-black, schools.

But the picture is not totally bleak. A few state legislatures have allocated sufficient fiscal resources to implement desegregation efforts. A few local school boards at the time of this writing have passed strong resolutions advocating desegregation. A few states have moved ahead in defining and establishing bilingual/bicultural programs. The Title IX Ethnic Heritage program is a step in the right direction.

The need for polycultural education becomes even more critical when we note the many urban health and educational programs being de-escalated and closed out. This is happening at a time when one out of five Chicano children is failing to enroll in school, when the mortality rate of America's first citizen, the Native American, is allowed to be double the national average, when the black male must still possess three years of college education in order to earn as much as his white counterpart with eight years of schooling, when two-thirds of the nation's poor children, who are white, continue to exist in poverty!

How then can a polycultural education contribute to improving the human condition of America's educational institutions? A polycultural curriculum can be the mechanism to re-educate students to higher levels of human understanding. This new level of understanding will permit educators and book publishers to begin reaching and teaching students about the true American experience through a broad range of learning materials. Such materials will address the everyday experiences of the racial, ethnic, and cultural groups that constitute the great potential promise of our nation. A polycultural education can contribute to the arrest of racial fears and hatred.

A polycultural education can facilitate the re-education of yesterday's generation through today's enlightened children. And when that re-education occurs Americans will understand why the city of Atlanta, in vigorous opposition to the NAACP, tabled school desegregation in exchange for black community empowerment. When that re-education occurs, white Americans will understand why desegregation is no longer blindly accepted by black people as a panacea for the achievement of black children. When that re-education occurs, Americans will understand why Chicano and Puerto Rican groups in New York City are demanding that curriculum materials be made more relevant. And when that re-education occurs minority groups will understand why white ethnic groups are demanding that the learning materials address the white ethnics who toiled in the fields, worked the steel mills, mined the hills, and cut the forests. The state of Michigan is to be commended for enacting legislation enabling the Michigan State Department of Education to re-examine the impact of racial and ethnic groups on American history.

And what about the feelings of educators and students? The following comments were taken from a newspaper article on school desegregation:

> *A black student:* "I would send my kids to an integrated school; then they would get to know and understand different kinds of people."
>
> *A white student:* "Yeah, the kids in this neighborhood who didn't go to school with black students are different—they're prejudiced. They call names and stuff, but not when they're around blacks, only when they're in the neighborhood—but, I guess the school thing is pretty good. I don't know what could be done to get people not to be prejudiced. Maybe just the school thing would do it."
>
> *A white counselor:* "We would like our students to have some sense of indentity, both personal and cultural, so when they come together they don't become just one big pot of mediocrity."[17]

A polycultural education can be the mechanism to cleanse educational institutions of racist/sexist literature and racist/sexist research studies. Much of the current racist-oriented literature bela-

---

[17]*Minneapolis Tribune,* May 12, 1974.

bors the failure of desegregation, the failure of poverty programs, and the failure of colonized, minority group children to achieve. The debates among educators go on, and the philosophic polarizations concomitant with such debates serve to embellish the social malady that is America's, the pollution of racism.

The subject of race and intelligence quotient is the great catalyst for educator discussions. And today we are witness to the most interesting sociopolitical alignments. Liberal sociologists side with the environmentalists. The IQ geneticists find company with the racists. Nationally acclaimed proponents of black colonization such as Arthur Jensen, David Armor, Christopher Jencks, Arthur Hernstein, and lately James Coleman in their spurious research findings have attempted to pick up a torch that even Gregor Mendel would have been wise enough to throw down. They have attempted to give an academic cloak of respectability to a racist mentality that suggests one race is genetically superior to another. They have conveniently disregarded such factors as the innate bias of middle-class created tests, physical environment, vitamin deficiencies, and inadequate educational programs. It is discomforting to see that studies refuting the conclusions of Jensen and Hernstein have been largely ignored. None of the major journals have seen fit to give significant coverage to the Milwaukee project directed by Dr. Rick Heber, nor to Dr. William Rower's positive findings entitled "Learning, Race and School Success." In the Milwaukee project, Dr. Heber concluded that the intervention of creative educational programs can arrest and reverse the retardation process of low-income black children. Every educator, parent, and lay citizen concerned with the survival of educationally cheated, colonized children should scrutinize the racist materials being published and promulgated today in the name of scholarly research.

Which way is America to go? Can the escalating racial, ethnic, cultural antagonisms be reversed? Are we destined to be a nation of separate nations? Can Americans—red, yellow, black, tan, and white—work together to transform the great phrase "one nation, under God, indivisible, with liberty and justice for all" into a reality for every American?

There is really nothing difficult about establishing an effective polycultural program. All it takes is a will, commitment, action, and resources. There is difficulty in getting some of the people within organizations to commit themselves sufficiently. That is the challenge for educators and education. And it must be clearly understood that without clear commitments by the organization (in clearly stated goals and objectives for a polycultural curriculum), the effort is defeated before it is begun.

## America Can and Will Choose Wisely Between Polycultural Education and Polycultural Conflict

The time is now for polycultural education! The destiny of this nation hinges upon the development of its most precious resource, our children and youth. The phenomena of racism and sexism in education must not continue to be the barriers to developing this precious resource. The implementation of a polycultural education in school organizations would be a major step toward removal of those barriers.

The racial, social, and cultural health of America must be revitalized, and now is the time to do it. The conscience of America, our physician, will set into motion a constructive diagnosis and prescription for cure. If this happens, future Americans may yet know its great promise: the freedom to live on a depolluted planet, the freedom to breathe depolluted air, the freedom to drink depolluted water, and the freedom to grow up together in a depolluted, racist-free society.

# BIBLIOGRAPHY

Banks, James A. "Teaching for Ethnic Literacy: A Comparative Approach." *Social Education* 37:738–50; December 1973.

Bennis, Warren G. "Changing Organizations." *The Journal of Applied Behavioral Science* 2:247–64; August–September 1966.

Bluck, Max. *The Social Theories of Talcott Parsons: A Critical Examination.* Englewood Cliffs, N.J.: Prentice-Hall, Inc., 1964.

Burke, Warner W., editor. *Contemporary Organization Development: Conceptual Orientations and Interventions.* Washington, D.C.: National Institute for Applied Behavioral Science, 1972.

Cass, James. "The Public Schools' Public." *The Saturday Review* 53:73; October 18, 1969.

Chrisman, Robert, and Hare, Nathan, editors. *Pan-Africanism.* New York: The Bobbs-Merrill Co., 1974.

Early, David F. "Promised Land for Moses." *Minneapolis Star,* April, 1974.

Ehlers, Henry J., editor, *Critical Issues in Education.* 5th edition. New York: Holt, Rinehart and Winston, 1973.

Esbensen, Thorwald. *Working with Individualized Instruction: The Duluth Experience.* Palo Alto, Calif.: Fearon Publishers, 1968.

Gagné, Robert M. "Curriculum Research and the Promotion of Learning." *Perspectives of Curriculum Evaluation,* American Educational Research Association Monograph Series on Curriculum Evaluation. (Series Editor, B. Othanel Smith.) Chicago: Rand McNally & Co., 1967. pp. 19–38.

Hersh, Semour M. "Racial Slurs Reportedly Made by Nixon." *Minneapolis Tribune,* May 12, 1974.

Macdonald, James B. "Curriculum Theory: Problems and a Prospectus." Address given at annual meeting of Professors of Curriculum, April 1964.

————. "The Person in the Curriculum." *Precedents and Promise in the Curriculum Field.* (Edited by H. F. Robison.) New York: Columbia Teachers College Press, 1966.

Maeger, Robert F. *Preparing Instructional Objectives.* Palo Alto, Calif.: Fearon Publishers, 1962.

Maslow, Abraham H. *Toward A Psychology of Being.* New York: Holt, Rinehart and Winston, 1962.

Miel, Alice. "Reassessment of the Curriculum—Why?" *A Reassessment of the Curriculum.* New York: Columbia Teachers College Press, 1964.

Minneapolis Tribune. "Here's How Desegregation Has Gone in Minneapolis." *Minneapolis Tribune,* May 11, 1974.

Moreland, J. Y. "History Texts Seldom Place Black Feats in Proper Perspective." *The Twin City Courier* (Minneapolis, Minn.), February, 1974.

Sulkin, Sidney. "Introduction." *The Challenge of Curriculum Change.* New York: College Entrance Examination Board, 1966.

Thomas, Henry. *Understanding the Great Philosophers.* New York: Doubleday and Co., Inc., 1962.

U.S. Department of Health, Education and Welfare, National Institute of Mental Health, Center for Minority Group Mental Health Programs. *Bibliography on Racism.* Rockville, Md.: the Center, 1972.

Wann, Kenneth D. "The Curriculum Field Today." *Precedents and Promise in the Curriculum Field.* (Edited by H. F. Robison.) New York: Columbia Teachers College Press, 1966.

Williams, Robert L. *Educational Alternatives for Colonized People: Models for Liberation.* New York: Dunellen Publishing Co., 1974.